Dogs and Their Women

Bambi Ann Baranski with Scooter and Wiley   PHOTO: John A. Baranski

Dogs and Their Women

Barbara Cohen and Louise Taylor

LITTLE, BROWN AND COMPANY

BOSTON   TORONTO   LONDON

FIRST EDITION

Library of Congress Cataloging-in-Publication Data
Cohen, Barbara, 1949–
    Dogs and their women / by Barbara Cohen and Louise Taylor. — 1st ed.
        p.   cm.
    ISBN 0-316-15036-3
    1. Dogs — Anecdotes.   2. Women dog owners — Anecdotes.   3. Dogs —
Pictorial works.   4. Women dog owners — Pictorial works.
I. Taylor, Louise, 1949–.   II. Title.
SF426.2.C64 1989
636.7 — dc 19   88-39993
                                                                            CIP

10 9 8 7 6 5 4 3

Designed by Robert G. Lowe

RRD-VA

Published simultaneously in Canada
by Little, Brown & Company (Canada) Limited

PRINTED IN THE UNITED STATES OF AMERICA

For our parents
Minna and Aaron,
Penny and Tiger

Acknowledgments

WE ARE EXTREMELY GRATEFUL to the hundreds of women who sent photographs and wrote such heartfelt letters to us about their dogs. *Dogs and Their Women* would never have been published without their interest and encouragement. We would like to thank Carol Ross for her unyielding support for the book and especially for designing the flyer, which got the project off the ground. We wish to thank Rose Marston, who initiated the first newspaper article about our efforts (for Beacon Communications), and Carol Stocker of the *Boston Globe*, whose feature article subsequently attracted hundreds of letters and photographs. Our gratitude goes to the late Jeremy Ross, who suggested the title, and to Michele Kort for her invaluable editing.

We wish to thank Roberta Vesley of the American Kennel Club Library for her assistance and research, the American Kennel Club, the Delta Society, the Dog Museum of America, St Hubert's Giralda, the Massachusetts Society for the Prevention of Cruelty to Animals, *Canine Collector's Companion, DOG FANCY, DOGworld,* the Humane Society of the United States, and *Pet Gazette.* For their support, encouragement, and assistance we would like to thank Paula Bennett, Gail Gordon, Frank Simpson, Marjorie Thompson, Mary Ann Krebs, Mary Dreshon, Norma Jacobs, Karen Krider, Judith Hoch, Pam White, Chris Triebert, Deirdre Grunwald, Lisa DeFrancis, Doe Coover, Vivienne Simon, the staff of the School of Programs in Management for Business and Industry at Lesley College, and the dog-loving women of Menauhant on Cape Cod. Considerable thanks go to Little, Brown and Company, to Jennifer Josephy, and especially to Sarah Pence.

For their love and support we thank our families. Much love to Eros for his years of devotion to Barbara and for the love he now gives Barbara's parents. Louise wishes to acknowledge her dogs, Eric, Heidi, and Hoden, who are now in heaven. Last we dedicate this book to our dogs, Gabe and Bentley, in gratitude for their patience and unconditional love.

Introduction

GROWING UP in the fifties, we watched "Rin Tin Tin" and "Lassie" on television and *Old Yeller* at the movies, all of which depicted relationships between boys and dogs. And dogs have always been "man's best friend." But we know that there is another side to the story. This book is a long-overdue celebration of the loving relationship that women have with their dogs. The combination of a dog's unconditional love and loyalty and a woman's nurturing invariably results in a deep emotional attachment. This closeness is a constant in a world with few guarantees and continual change. As Eve Minson describes it, women's unique bond with their dogs honors them as equals. She explains, "I don't consider the dogs as my pets, it's more that we're all fortunate to be sharing the same rocky road."

Our first conversation was about our dogs. We soon discovered that each of us had had thoughts about creating a special book to describe in words and pictures what we felt for our dogs. Barbara, years ago in California, pondered a book of unique dog stories, while Louise, on the East Coast, envisioned a book of portraits of women and their dogs. With the mailing of a hand-drawn flyer to friends on either coast and a few veterinary clinics, the impetus for *Dogs and Their Women* grew. Encouraged by the heartfelt letters and snapshots this initial effort brought, we turned to the media for broader publicity. A major feature in the *Boston Globe* and a new, updated, flyer later, we were struggling to keep up with personal responses to each letter and photo we received. Finally, from more than 500 photographs and wonderful stories, we shaped this book to convey the wide range of emotions, personalities, and experiences that make up the world of dogs and women. It is a journey through all ages and life-styles.

The following pages will introduce you to Paula, who at thirteen wrote about her dog Topper that "he was the only thing I loved. And just as important, he was the only thing I let love me." And Jo Giese, who "replaced a six-foot Swedish husband with a five-pound dog." Althea Griffin, "six months a widow [and finding her] empty home unbearable," filled the

Barbara Cohen and Louise Taylor
with Gabe and Bentley

PHOTO: © Rose Marston

ix

void by adopting Mandy, a stray, who had been "confined to a cramped cage for six weeks with her eight newborn puppies." You'll meet Daisy Mae, a "singularly undemure" bloodhound, whose loving owner "could not resist the juxtaposition of her femme fatale nomenclature with her incongruous presence."

Also here are the women who receive greater gifts than love from their dogs, like eight-year-old Melissa, whose "best friend" is her golden retriever, Cashew. "He turns off the lights when we leave the room to go for a walk and pulls me in my wheelchair." Helen Keller wrote of "the love which impels [dogs] to break their silence about me with . . . news conveyed by expressive ear, nose and paw." Marcia Koenig, who works with her dog, Bear, searching for people lost in the wilderness, recognizes that "our partnership is greater than either of our individual abilities." Ann Bancroft, an Arctic explorer, would agree. Speaking of her favorite sled dog, Sam, she writes: "We needed each other to get to the top of the world."

Thirteen years ago Barbara found her first dog in a cardboard box. "When I found Eros it was as though something had instantly filled this empty space in my heart." Louise grew up with a sequence of large dogs including a Great Dane, a German shepherd, and a golden retriever. "Although I loved all of the dogs from my youth, Hoden, my black Lab/shepherd was my favorite. He exemplifies the meaning of this book — he was always there."

Dogs and Their Women

Once they love, they love steadily, unchangingly, till their last breath.
That is how I like to be loved.
Therefore I will write of dogs.

Elizabeth,
All the Dogs of My Life, 1936

WE BONDED the moment Mandy was released from her small cage at the dog pound in November 1974. Six months a widow, I had found my empty home unbearable. Adopting Mandy was my answer, and I became her savior as well. She had been confined to a cramped cage for six weeks with her eight newborn puppies. She was malnourished and dehydrated. The steadfast love and loyalty we have given each other has been a quiet joy unlike any other!

PHOTO: Everett Tatreau   *Althea Griffin and Mandy*

Dodger is my best friend. I love him because he gives me lots of licks in the face.

Photo: Tom Glinka

Alexandra Glinka and Dodger

DAISY MAE SEEMS AN ABSURD NAME for a dog so singularly undemure. I must confess that I did not name her but was so amused when we first met (she was eight months old and already weighed ninety pounds) that I could not resist the juxtaposition of her femme fatale nomenclature with her incongruous presence.

Daisy is lovable, gentle, and adores children and babies. Unfortunately she is also stubborn and uneducable with a mind of her own. This is due in part to the fact that, being a hound, she tends to be a victim of her nose. She is completely obsessed with food and has to be perpetually on a diet. Daisy's other pastimes include sleeping on her futon and drooling. (Bloodhounds are not for the squeamish.) Another distinguishing feature is that she rarely barks. Instead, she bays, much to the chagrin of some neighbors, who are convinced there is a cow in labor in their midst. I, however, find her quite melodious.

Contrary to popular belief, bloodhounds are not named for their tracking ability, nor for their bloodshot eyes. Rather, they are the "blooded" hounds of the royal families of historical Europe. This, then, is the source of Daisy's dignified countenance. I am constantly amazed when strangers misinterpret her facial expression as depression. Nothing could be farther from the truth. Daisy is ecstatic in her own way; it's just that bloodhounds aren't effusive.

PHOTO: John Dawson   *Judith Posner and Daisy Mae*

THIS IS ME WITH MY DOG, TOPPER, in the spring of 1950. I was thirteen and a half and desperately unhappy. We lived in a nice house on a nice street in a nice suburb outside of Boston. I went to private school. I was on the verge of flunking out and did the following year. I had no friends to speak of. I lived in a private world: the woods behind our house, my books, my fantasies, and my dog. I built this world originally to keep my mother out. I had been living in it ever since I could remember; hating people, wanting only to be left alone. I can't prove Topper helped me survive those years. I don't know what would have happened if he had not been there. But I do know he was the only thing I loved. And just as important, he was the only thing I let love me.

PHOTO: Ursula Bernath   *Paula Bennett and Topper*

I FOUND JACK in a parking lot. Or he found me. I had no trouble getting him to come home with me. Open your tailgate and he'd follow you anywhere. One might say he loved going for rides, but that would be a severe understatement, since he would become a dervish at the jangle of keys.

Sarah and Jack

BEAR HAS BEEN A SEARCH DOG, trained to look for lost people in the wilderness, his entire life. In this photo we were flying in West Texas in search of a lost elderly person.

I started training him at nine weeks, and now, at eleven years, he'd rather be out in the woods searching than anything else. Bear is the best search dog I've ever had and also the most difficult. I suspect the two go together. He is very assertive and tests me periodically to see if I'm willing to give up leadership of the pack to him. His assertiveness enables him to range farther than most dogs and to think for himself, not allowing me to call him off a scent.

My greatest satisfaction in working with Bear comes from the knowledge that our partnership is greater than either of our individual abilities. I decide how to cover our area, taking advantage of terrain and wind. Bear searches for the scent of a human being. We have been partners for so long now that I don't say much when we're on a search. He reads my body language to know where he is to go, and I read his to know what he's doing. I also get pleasure just watching Bear and the enjoyment he gets from being out in the woods, freely ranging, exploring, and hunting for the lost person. There is a wonderful rapport that comes from working with Bear, knowing that we have the possibility of saving a person's life.

PHOTO: Bob Koenig

Marcia Koenig and Bear

G<small>ET CRACKING</small>, Shirley, or we won't end together.

Shirley Mae Ross and Fritz

ONE summer I lived alone with my dogs on a small island off the coast of Maine. I had made a trip to the mainland without them, and it was late at night; the fog and drizzle were thick as I motored out of the harbor. I tried following the lobster markers, but that became impossible as the sea swells grew larger. Finally, I could not see beyond the bow of the boat and I had to rely on my sense of direction, as there was no compass on the boat! Suddenly, I knew I had overshot the island. To collect my thoughts, I put the motor into neutral. By mistake, I hit the choke and the engine died! I tried to start the motor, but it would not cooperate. I tried again. I slumped down into the seat and dissolved into tears. My boat sloshed about, with water pouring over the sides. I then let out a frantic call for help.

What make animals sense danger or trouble long before human beings react? I am certain that by the time I cried out, Ursa was already in the water. From the rocks she plunged into that black, cold, angry water, with only her instincts to guide her. At first I heard her bark and thought she was on land, so I called her name over and over, trying to paddle the boat in her direction. Then my light caught her brown eyes riveted on me. She swam up to the boat, whining with concern for me. As I reached over to help hold her up to rest, she kept trying to grab my old canvas hat, which she always wanted to carry when I came back to the island from a jaunt. I frantically tied it to the painter, shoved it in her mouth, and yelled, "Let's go home, Ursa!" I gave the motor one more chance — and it caught!

Ursa swam ahead of my boat, just within the circle of my light, but the going was tedious. I became so discouraged when she finally refused to swim any further. Holding her tightly in my arms, crying into her wet, salty fur to tell her it was okay, I was struck on the side of the head by the big white mooring ball. No wonder she wouldn't swim anymore. Ursa had brought me home.

Ursa met an untimely and tragic death soon after she saved my life, but to this day I have never been without a Newf, as the photo proves.

PHOTO: David Allen   *Betsy Weiderhold with Dory, Breeze, and Paw Paw*

WHEN IT CAME TIME to plan my wedding (a private ceremony in the woods), there was no question about who would play all the "extra" parts. Oboe served as maid of honor, flower girl, best man, and the one who gave me away.

All this — just for a chance to kiss the bride!

PHOTO: © Sharon A. Bazarian

Christy Fajkowski and Oboe

BARNEY COMES EVERY DAY to the college art museum I direct. We are in an austere, postmodern building; it is painted white and hung with an extraordinary collection of art. The casual visitor, entering the doors, could be awestruck, literally cowed by the formality of the architectural setting and the greatness of the works of art.

Then Barney peeks his long beagle nose around the corner, or rolls over as he sleeps under the Degas. Immediately the visitor knows this is a friendly, informal place. Barney's business card reads "Security and Social Director." Here is a dog of many talents but few teeth.

PHOTO: John M. Ewing

Judith Sobol and Barney

IT TAKES about forty-five minutes to get to the park from our house. Thirty-five minutes into the journey there's a sudden burst of excitement and commotion in my van. Tails start pounding loudly against the metal sides, noses smear the glass steamed with dog breath. Circling, fussing, and whining build to a crescendo. It amazes me every time how they carry on like this at the exact same spot along the road. I wonder if they recognize the trees or the houses or the smell of the woods, or if they simply know we're getting closer because they can read my mind.

PHOTO: © Judith Hoch

Lee Holmes with Roxie and Zorro

Dear Friends

I want to tell you about my best friend, his name is Cashew He is a big and smart golden-retreiver and can do lots of things for me like pick up my pencils when I drope them and he brings me my dolls and he is always picking up my shoes. He turns off the lights when we leave the room to go for a walk and pulls me in my wheel-chair. He is fun to go shopping with, which I could never do before. We play ball and have fun together and we love each other very much.

McLissa

Courtesy of Canine Companions for Independence (CCI), P.O. Box 446, Santa Rosa, CA 95402. CCI is a nonprofit organization funded solely by private donations. Melissa, at age eight, was the first female child to receive a Canine Companion Service dog.

Melissa and Cashew

PEOPLE TELL US we look more like sisters than mother and daughter.

PHOTO: © G. Robert Bishop

Jeri Wagner and Sasha

MISS BADGER'S MOTHER, a black Lab with a pedigree, had an early, illicit affair with the boy next door. Although Badg outgrew her mother in size and in swimming skills, her long silky ears are a heritage from the neighbor's beagle.

Miss Badger is a farm dog. She keeps coons, woodchucks, and rabbits out of the gardens. Her bark alerts me to cars and her growls warn strangers to keep their distance. But Badg is a marshmallow, a patient, gentle, malleable creature with my small grandchildren who, poor dears, are growing up in dogless homes.

Miss Badger can be eighty-five pounds of well-mannered dignity when my living room is filled with guests. She's a serious work dog on her daily farm patrols. But, when I put on my old brown jacket, Badg prances like a pup and chases herself in circles in anticipation of a sniffing, racing exploration through the woods.

When I comb Miss Badger out on the lawn, the hair she sheds is put in under the hemlocks. Badg and I watch the birds carry this off to weave into their nests.

To live in the country without a dog would be like visiting an art gallery wearing a blindfold. Miss Badger's senses of smells and sounds lead me to daily discoveries. She has called me to view a tiny pistachio-colored snake, the fattest toad in the county, and deer on the lawn in the moonlight. Badg is endlessly curious. I'm learning that rewarding quality.

PHOTO: Neal Parent   *Arley Carman Clark and Miss Badger*

GERALDINE R. DODGE was an ardent supporter of animal welfare and the foremost purebred dog fancier of her generation. Her Giralda Farms Kennels produced hundreds of champions from 1927 through 1965. She conceived and hosted the renowned Morris and Essex Dog Show, from 1927 through 1957, which was considered to be the finest and largest outdoor show in the world. In 1933, she became the first woman to judge best of show at Westminster. A well-respected all-breed judge, she wrote books on her two favorite breeds, the German shepherd and English cocker spaniel. Her five-acre kennel site housed one hundred twenty-five dogs, but she always kept eight to ten dogs in the house. These were usually dogs that did not meet the confirmation standards for their breed and would not be shown competitively. In her lifetime she owned more than eighty breeds of dogs.

In 1939, she founded St. Hubert's Giralda Animal Welfare and Education Center, which rescues more than three thousand stray dogs and cats annually and reaches 120,000 children per year through its educational programs. St. Hubert's has received national accreditation from the Humane Society of the United States and the American Humane Association for its excellent standards of operation.

Courtesy of Edwin J. Sayres, St. Hubert's Giralda

Geraldine R. Dodge, 1882–1973

I HOLD HIM BACK for a moment; anticipation ripples through his body. Sea gulls keep their distance, eyeing him with caution, waiting for the moment when I let him go. They will scatter in every direction and some will circle back, flying low to tease him as he chases their shadows, sometimes nipping at the sand. Oh how we loved this game.

PHOTO: Vilnis Ruicis

Mary Ann Krebs and Riddle

THIS PHOTOGRAPH was taken at the north pole. There are many pictures of the six human team members at the top of the world, but this is the only one I have seen honoring the dogs who were the unsung heroes of that journey. Quite plainly, we could not have made it without them. This photograph is one of my favorites, because Sam and I really had to hang in there together and help each other to reach our destination.

Sam was a wild dog that Richard Weber, of the Steger International Polar Expedition, caught on a training trip. He has been pulling with relish ever since. The team, however, never accepted him. At times I, too, felt like an outcast being, for so many months, the only woman on the expedition. Our immediate bond seemed to make perfect sense.

We took care of each other throughout the training and the trip. The nurturing and warmth that I missed so much were unconditionally given by Sam. I would share my rations with him and make sure he got plenty of loving and a safe bed away from the team. One day when I was running the team, I left them momentarily to help another sled that was stuck. Once I was out of sight, the team attacked Sam. I heard the fight, ran back, and jumped into the frenzy, fists flying. Sam did not come out of the fight unscathed. Crying and cussing at the others, I checked him out and decided not to keep him in harness. As he stiffened up, I tried to share my lunch with him, but he would not take it. At night I took him far from the team, nursed his wounds, fed him antibiotics, and wrapped him in my parka. Each day I would talk to him and coax him to walk and eat, and beg him not to leave me to this journey alone.

He did heal in time to be chosen as one of the twenty going all the way to the pole. We needed each other to get to the top of the world.

PHOTO: Sam Cook

Ann E. Bancroft and Sam

Hᴇʀ ɴᴀᴍᴇ was Mesa Louise Yazzie. I found her dying in a ditch on the Navajo Reservation. She had never had a person. Half wild, she had a punctured lung and was a walking skeleton. After a treatment from the closest vet (100 miles away), she began healing. She became my best friend and was very devoted and protective of me. Within the first week of my knowing her an amazing thing happened. I was lying in bed reading and she was lying on the foot of the bed (in her bandages). She got up and deliberately walked up to me and placed her cheek next to mine. She held it there for a minute or two in a gesture that told me our friendship was sealed. She died in 1975. I buried her in a mountain meadow of the San Francisco Peaks, holy to both the Navajo and Hopi. It was where she and I used to go and watch the Arizona sunsets. What a pure little spirit she was.

Pʜᴏᴛᴏ: Marilyn Steiner Sano

Paula Gray and Mesa Louise Yazzie

JAKE is a pet-therapy dog. His career started with a woman named Rose Sickles. Rose is a woman in her eighties, whose life began to crumble several years ago. She had lived alone for many years, but eventually her health deteriorated and she could no longer take care of herself. She had been sent by her family to the Prospect Park Nursing Home in Brooklyn, New York, and she hated it. She was cantankerous, uncooperative, and bitter. She threw her food at her nurses. She hated them and the other patients and was angry with her family. She wanted her apartment back and, most important, her independence, which she could not accept as lost forever.

And then she was introduced to Jake. Still a puppy, he immediately adored Rose, and the feeling was mutual. Rose would save little pieces of food for Jake's next visit, and of course that cemented their friendship.

Rose began to tell the nurses she was only living to see Jake. She said she waited twenty-nine days for the thirtieth, when Jake would come. Soon Jake spent the entire time at the nursing home with Rose rather than circulating with the other residents.

For the first year she didn't talk to me. She would just tell Jake how she hated being there, how the food was bad, and she would feed him cookies the whole time. One day she looked at me and said, "Do you want a cookie?" Now she talks to me about her life, and the dogs she owned.

PHOTO: Janice Braverman
Courtesy of Micky Niego, Jill Schensul, and the ASPCA

Rose Sickles and Jake

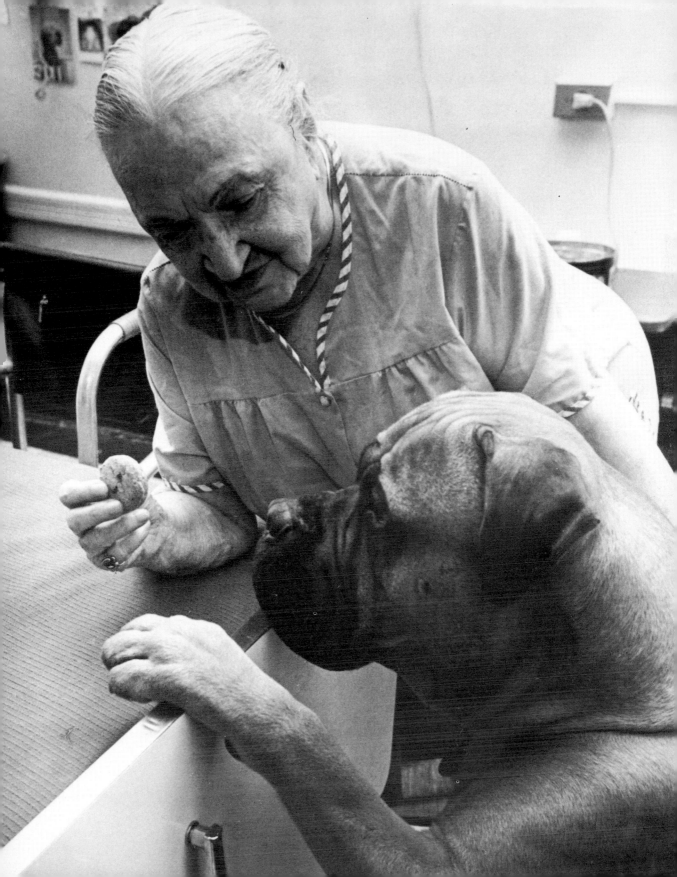

I ONLY HAD TO SHOW HIM ONCE and he knew it would be fun.

PHOTO: Dean F. Claussen, Jr.

Elaine K. Claussen and Chance of Thunder

AND SO THERE WE WERE, on our steps, as though we were waiting for the parade to go by our house on Fenwick Road. Jane, Laura, and Gail, and of course, our beloved dog, Maeve. She looked so dignified and thoughtful as she waited with us, knowing in her own intuitive way that something very special was about to happen.

PHOTO: H. Gugenheimer

Jane, Laura, and Gail Kronheim with Maeve, 1953

SASHA IS THE FIRST DOG I ever lived with. Although she excelled in her first swimming lesson, her roommate skills leave something to be desired. She helps sort the laundry by pulling clothes out of the dryer/basket (usually socks) and scattering them around the house. She cleans up after dinner whenever I let her and sometimes when I haven't asked for help. She assists with my gardening by digging holes for bulb planting, although most times in places I never thought to plant.

Sasha is also a friend and a teacher. She listens but doesn't interrupt. She comforts me when I am sad, hugging me in her own way, with a paw, nose, or a wiggle of her body. She knows how to forgive and forget, and how to make friends with everyone, not just her own kind. She is spontaneous and finds joy in simple things. I treasure Sasha's natural qualities — she makes me a finer person.

Colleen Macdonald and Sasha

Evolution of a Dog's Name

Patrick

Petrucchio

Trucchio

Truko

Truke Duke

Duke of Dogs

Duke

Duck

Duckie

Ducko

Doog

Doog Mahn

Doogalo

Woovalo

Wover

Woovie

Woovs

Wulfie

Wulf

Fulf

Fluff

Fluffie

Fluff Bucket

Flem Face

Farfell

Farflea

Fleabone

Farflono

Farfleato

Flotty

Flots

Flowtron

Flottie

Aeroflot

Bowzer

Beasto

Beasty

Beastly

Sweet Beast

Sweetie Cheeks

Snuggle Bunny

PHOTO: Per O. Hoel

Ana Hoel and Patrick

On our outings at the beach, my mother delights in seeing my dachshund, Frank, swim. As she holds him above the waves he kicks his short legs left, right, left, right — like a small turtle. Using his tail as a rudder, he splashes through the surf with his head held high. It's only his sparkling brown eyes and long floating ears that distinguish him from a reddish brown log washing onto the beach.

Photo: C. Leigh Farmer

Elizabeth Farmer and Frank

ONE DAY I arrived home to hear my next door neighbor screaming, "Your dog has killed my cat!" From a distance I could see Gretchen's body wrapped around the motionless cat. I thought the worst had actually happened, until I got a closer look. The cat was sleeping peacefully, protected by Gretchen's paws and her maternal instincts. Gretchen is as loving and intelligent as she is beautiful. She completely shatters the typical Doberman image.

PHOTO: Andrew Jay Heller

Jude Hartley and Gretchen

THE CHARMING RELATIONS I have had with a long succession of dogs results from their happy spontaneity. Usually they are quick to discover that I can not see or hear. Considerately they rise as I come near, so that I may not stumble. It is not a training but love which impels them to break their silence about me with the thud of a tail rippling against my chair, or gambols round the study, or news conveyed by expressive ear, nose and paw. Often I yearn to give them speech, their motions are so eloquent with things they can not say. Truly, as companions, friends, equals in opportunities of self-expression, they unfold to me the dignity of creation, and their joy smiles the blessing of St. Francis.

— Helen Keller, *A Tribute to a Dog*

Helen Keller and Polly Thompson with Kenzan-Go

I WASN'T LOOKING for a dog when I got Jake, I was looking for a friend.

PHOTO: © R. Gregoire   *Karen Krider and Jake*

WHEN SNOWFLAKE WAS A PUPPY she reminded me of a snowflake dancing and skipping about, as she stole my best nightgown from the laundry and went running gaily through the living room. She knew my every move and gesture. When I was reading a book she'd hop on my lap and curl up, and I'd use her rump as a book stand. When I'd get ready to go to bed she'd hop on the pillow next to mine, and that's where she slept all of her fifteen years. Snowflake saw me through some very difficult times. The comfort she gave me was a blessing. She calmed my every fear — my beloved Snowflake, my precious friend forever.

PHOTO: Melvin F. Hookailo, M. Photog., Cr., A.S.P., CPP   *Bernadine J. Scutta and Snowflake*

RUBEN AND BUSTER are the definitive odd couple, one being six pounds and the other one hundred twenty-five pounds. They are soul mates and at times inspiration for my paintings. I have to admit that for this photo I had a piece of cheese in my hand, so Ruben turned into an exploding cigar, while Buster was his usual goody-two-shoes self.

PHOTO: Marva Morrow from *Inside the L.A. Artist.*
Peregrine Smith Books, 1988.

Victoria A. Nodiff with Ruben and Buster

58

OTIS IS THE HAPPIEST, sweetest, goofiest, most carefree and affectionate dog I've ever known. We look into each other's eyes, and I can both feel his deep love for me and know that he understands my devotion to him.

I often think about the fact that his expected life span is shorter than mine. One day of his life is equal to one week of mine. I am aware of how important it is to spend quality time with him every day, doing the things he loves to do — chasing balls, swimming, or just taking long walks in the woods.

The only time Otis is unhappy is when he sees my suitcase. He gets very low to the ground, flat as a pancake, and sulks until I convince him he's coming with me, which usually means letting him sit in the car long before I'm actually ready to go. The truth is, if Otis isn't coming with me, I'm as unhappy as he is.

PHOTO: © Alison Shaw

Gail Leeds and Otis

IN PRISON time is endless, yet with a dog to love, time has meaning.

Some people thought I was tough — but little Billy didn't, he knows my heart.

PHOTO: Sister Pauline (formerly Kathy Quinn)

Marina Chauvaud and Billy

DEVYN measures thirty-five inches at the shoulders, stands approximately six feet on his hind legs, and weighs about one hundred eighty pounds. He is as gentle and loving as he is huge.

He loves his food and just about anything you feed him, but buttered popcorn makes his eyes sparkle. He is also afflicted with a special disease called "tongue-dropsy," which means that his tongue will automatically drop into coffee cups, milk or pop glasses, and bowls of apple sauce.

PHOTO: Jacqueline S. Walker

Donna Walker and Devyn

HI, GIRLS! Oh, I'm so glad to see you too! Oh, what good girls! Yes —
yes, I love you too! Yes — yes, I missed you too. Yes, I'm home for the
evening now. Mmm, such nice kisses. Thank you. Thank you. Yes — good
girls. Oh, such nice kisses. I love you too.

PHOTO: Carl Socolow

Pam Williams, Sasha, and Tammy

I AWOKE and realized that somehow I had reached a decision. I would put her to sleep that day, I was ready to let her go. I turned and told her. I said I was quite reluctant to take this life-death matter into my own hands, so if, perchance, she felt she could do it, well, that would be much better.

I then noticed that it had begun to drizzle, one of those sweet warm summer sprinkles. I thought how she'd love to smell it. I gingerly picked her up and walked onto the porch with her in my arms. She lifted her head, twitching her nose. We stood there about a minute or so, the two of us sniffing the air, and then she died.

PHOTO: Paul Holzman   *Laurie Kaslow and Khyber*

IN HONOR of Buzzsaw's first birthday, I decided to have our picture taken. When we arrived at the photography studio, I'll admit I was a little nervous. Buzz often explores a new space with enthusiasm akin to a white tornado. Seeing her head like an anvil and her stout muscular body, people usually gather up their personal belongings and head for the closest exit. Amazingly, she behaved quite differently that day. She seemed to feel perfectly at home. After a perfunctory look/sniff, she strolled over to the seamless backdrop and flopped down. As the shoot progressed, she became so relaxed we couldn't even get her to stand up.

One of the best things about my relationship with Buzzsaw is the greeting she gives me at the end of each working day. From the moment my key touches the lock and I hear her hit the floor upstairs to when I'm finally sitting down reading the paper — with Buzz sighing and snoring beside me, one paw wrapped around my leg — we are both truly content. Nobody else has ever been that happy to see me.

PHOTO: Monica Lee

Alix Smith and Buzzsaw

M<small>Y DOG</small> T<small>OBY</small> was born on August 21, 1972, and died of old age on November 15, 1985.

Toby went with me to the store, the library, the bank — in fact, he went everywhere with me, except when I made a trip out of town. When I returned he would be waiting for me at the window, poking his nose through the curtains.

I buried him with a very special stone in my backyard. The forget-me-nots come up there every year. I've adopted a stray cat and I started to collect teddy bears, but it's Toby I really miss.

P<small>HOTO</small>: Margie Arnold

Anna Farquhar and Toby

As a young teenager, when girls my age were enjoying friends, school, and growing up, I was living in various institutions. I constantly ran away from home to avoid all of the fighting, pain, and conflict.

I sought comfort by visiting pet shops and looking at the animals. One day I bought *DOGworld* magazine and looked up all of the German shepherd kennels. I wrote to several, telling them that I was looking for a friend. A kennel in Texas responded and sent me a beautiful German shepherd named Jony, who became my constant companion. No longer did the police pick me up and put me away. I loved Jony so much that I wanted more friends and was given Dena and Chief.

Now, when I walked down the street with three beautiful shepherds, people would stop to ask about the dogs. That gave me an opportunity to communicate with people about a subject I knew and loved. I noticed that people started to change their attitude about me, and in time, great changes came to my life. I gained more self-confidence and learned how to train dogs. In 1967 I took my three dogs and joined a friend with her dogs and traveled across the United States, walking, hitch-hiking, and riding in freight trains. The photograph was taken during that journey, which took us four months.

My experience with dogs gave me the idea of starting a pilot project at Purdy State Prison to teach women inmates how to train dogs to help the handicapped. An inmate who trained the first dog for a disabled person said, "Having access to these dogs has helped me to realize that I am still capable of responding to living creatures and has put me in touch with feelings I was sure I had lost."

I know the pain of rejection, isolation, and loneliness, and I know that there are so many people who need to feel loved. Many can't trust, so the unconditional love that comes from the dog is ideal in reaching wounded souls.

Courtesy of Sister Pauline and Billie Broadus
Photo: © 1967 The *State Journal-Register*

Sister Pauline (formerly Kathy Quinn)
and the late Pat Broadus with Jony, Dena,
Chief, Sergeant, and Corporal

SULKI AND I love to take walks along this beautiful point of land on the oceanfront. I feel such a deep sense of safety and tranquility as she accompanies me — as if this were one of the ultimate gifts that life has to offer — love, so simple, silent, and complete.

Marilyn Steele and Sulki

HERE'S BUSBY AND JANE in the campaign photo we had done for our reelection to Hampton, New Hampshire, Town Clerk and Deputy. No one filed against us. How could they?

This dog makes me crazy, makes me exercise at 5:30 A.M. I loathe walking, and Busby literally pulls all one hundred ninety-three pounds of me. He weighs sixteen pounds and is total muscle. He takes my socks off at night and won't come when he's called. He has flunked dog classes twice but has had rottweilers and Newfoundlands cowering in the corners. He was in a terrier show in New Hampshire (very snooty) and when the judge tried to count his testicles, he bit her on the arm and was thrown out of the conformation class. I finally spent $314 sending him to private boarding school to teach him to come when he's called, but he got kennel cough instead. He's my pal, and gone are the long sequestered weekends of reading. Now it's trips and open windows in the car. There's hair everywhere. He eats better than I do and sleeps in the middle of my twin bed, while my extremities hang over the side onto the floor.

He loves me, balloons, dried apricots, grapes, apples, cats, people, women with fur sleeves, going to the dump in my truck and telling off three thousand sea gulls who live there. He's the most affectionate and wildest dog I ever had. I was going to have him fixed but discovered a perfect heart-shaped freckle on his weenie. I felt it was a sign that he is a lover and decided to leave him alone.

Jane Kelley and Busby

My LIFE WITH KATIE (on right) began when I was a second-year veterinary student in 1975. I first saw her in the small-animal clinic of the University of Georgia, College of Veterinary Medicine. She was a slender, sleek young Labrador retriever that had been donated to the school because she had X-ray evidence of hip dysplasia. We fell in love with each other and she came home with me. During the next two years, Katie helped me through school by having many of the problems I was studying.

After graduation I went on to do a specialty internship and residency. That meant traveling from Georgia to the state of Washington, from Washington to Michigan, and Michigan to New York. Finally we settled in Massachusetts. Katie was my companion during all of these travels. As long as she was with me, she was happy. She was my family while I was away from home.

Allie Alleyoop became part of this family in 1985. Katie was getting old and crippled and I was afraid that I needed another dog to cushion the blow when I lost her. Introducing Allie into our house was like letting in a hurricane. The best word to describe her is exuberant. She gives you the feeling that she is constantly laughing and smiling at the world.

Kate and Allie got along like the best of friends. Katie appeared to become younger overnight. I honestly feel that Allie prolonged Kate's life for another two years. Unfortunately I lost Katie to cancer in the summer of 1987. It was the end of a certain era of my life. I'll always remember her with deep affection, because she was my best friend during a time when I was so transient.

Allie doesn't replace Kate, but she certainly keeps me from taking life too seriously. It is very difficult to be unhappy when this eternal puppy is overflowing with the joy of life.

PHOTO: Margie Arnold

Mary Rose Paradis with Katie and Allie

I BELIEVE THAT TRAINING BRISTOL was the most loving gift that I could give her.

Terri Herigstad and Bristol

Gurry (the one on the right) died a year after this photo was taken. He devoted the thirteen years of his life to me. There couldn't have been a more gentle and loving dog. He once brought me a live mouse in his soft, crooked lips without harming it a bit.

I couldn't believe that another dog could take his place, but Otis, his son, is every bit as wonderful. Hopefully he will have a little more sense than Gurry and will stay out from under the horses and keep his face symmetrical — although there's a lot of character in that old, crooked face.

Now Otis is getting the wrinkly brow like his Dad — the "worried man" genes are showing through.

Photo: David Allen

Betsey MacDonald with Otis and Gurry

WILLIE G., ALIAS FURBALL, COTTONWAD, OR PUPPER, is one great little dog. She inspired me to start the world's largest dog/owner fun-run series and also to write *Running with Man's Best Friend.*

It took me two weeks to teach her this pose. (Bet you thought she was really stretching.) We practiced against the dining room wall. She probably thought it was the silliest trick I ever taught her.

PHOTO: E. Joe Deering

Davia Gallup and Willie

WHEN does a conscientious dog owner turn to a dog psychologist? Miko Tai Li, my incredibly wonderful Chinese Shar Pei delivered a handsome litter of six in 1985. Prior to delivery and all during nursing, veterinary trips, etc., a toy alligator had become part of the litter. When Miko took walks outside she would gently carry the alligator with her, then bring it back with her to the whelping box.

The following year Miko began nesting with the alligator and five other toy animals, including a teddy bear, dinosaur, hippopotamus, Dumbo the elephant, and a rabbit. She had acquired these animals at her birthday parties as gifts from her other dog friends. Not understanding the dynamics of what was happening, I consulted Miko's obstetrician, who referred me to a dog behaviorist. She exclaimed "What a nice size litter," and alerted me to the fact that Miko had had a false pregnancy. The veterinarian advised me to allow her to "attend" to her "pups" in order to keep her from going into a depression.

At the end of the nursing period Miko was living with her natural daughter Ch'ien (from her real litter), her six toys, and me, her human mother, who really wasn't quite sure who anyone was at that point. Now when does a dog owner consult her psychologist?

Nancy Sawdon with Miko Tai Li and Ch'ien Li

I WANTED A BIG RUGGED DOG, not a petite lapdog. But Charly insists on sitting in my lap even though he outweighs me. Cuddling with him, I can relax and let our love for each other replace the cares of the day. I'm glad Charly doesn't know he isn't a Pekinese.

PHOTO: © Judith Hoch

Cathy Robinowitz and Charlemagne

Dorothy Eustis, a wealthy Philadelphian, lived in Vevey, Switzerland, in the 1920s, where she trained German shepherds as work dogs for the Swiss army, the Swiss police, and the Red Cross.

In 1927, Mrs. Eustis was asked to write an article for the *Saturday Evening Post* about her work. Fearing that people in the United States would write and ask to buy her dogs, she instead wrote about a place in Potsdam, Germany, where German shepherds were being trained to lead blinded World War I veterans. She called the article "The Seeing Eye" after the verse in Proverbs that reads: "The seeing eye and the hearing ear, the Lord hath made even both of them."

Much to her surprise, she received volumes of mail from blind Americans who wanted to know if she could provide them with trained guide dogs. She was particularly moved by a letter from a blind man from Nashville, Tennessee, named Morris Frank.

Mrs. Eustis invited Mr. Frank to Switzerland to work with a dog, and on returning to the United States, he demonstrated the abilities of his dog, Buddy, who became the first Seeing Eye dog. Two years later, Mrs. Eustis returned to the United States, and The Seeing Eye, a place where dogs would be trained to guide blind people and the blind would learn to work with guide dogs, was founded in Nashville, Tennessee, on January 29, 1929. The school subsequently moved to Morristown, New Jersey, where it continues its valuable work today.

Dorothy Eustis: Founder of The Seeing Eye®

A FORMER GRADE A RACER, Touch would have been destroyed because of an injury incurred while racing, had I not adopted him.

I remember the day we brought him home. After living six years in a kennel he had never encountered stairs. We had to carry him (all ninety pounds) up two flights. He walked in, looked around, and immediately curled up on the couch. At six years of age, this was his first opportunity to live the life of a family pet and no longer that of a racing machine. I believe that the extreme loyalty of greyhounds stems from their past suffering. They are truly thankful to be alive.

PHOTO: © Judith Hoch

Linda Peterson and Touch

BEAR, a black chow, used to wander through my yard at times. She avoided all of my attempts at friendly interaction, but I always thought she was lovely. When a friend told me that Bear had had puppies and that her owner was trying to find a home for one, we rushed over to Bear's place. The owner was not at home, but I could see the puppy, who was about twelve weeks old at the time and irresistible. I was so excited, I climbed over the fence to get close to the puppy. I picked her up, and she put her paws around my neck. I have been in heaven ever since.

Joyce Nordquist and Tuffy McChow

SINCE HE ARRIVED, unannounced and unexpected, eight years ago, Elijah has been in the center of my life. My boyfriend came to live with me in Colorado during my freshman year of college and brought along an eight-week-old companion. Elijah made the two of us a family and was a tangible reminder of the island on the East Coast where Glen and I had met and Elijah was born.

I still like to think that Elijah is happiest on his native ground. Some of my favorite times with him are the trips that the two of us make alone to Block Island. His face lights up when I tell him where we're headed, that the beach is waiting, his favorite pond. He never fails to receive praise on the ferry as he sits on the bench beside me, nose to the wind, from less fortunate owners whose dogs are cowering and shaking beneath their legs. When we finally reach the sand road to the house, and the leash is off, my heart races up the hill with him, flushing pheasants, sniffing at deer trails, and running for the sheer love of it. Evening finds us on the back porch, listening to the crickets and smelling the night air.

People have teased me about spoiling Elijah, taking him with me everywhere I go, letting him share my ice cream cones or sleep under the covers, but I know they just haven't been lucky enough to experience the love that we share. Knowing how important my happiness is to him makes me glad for the little ways I can show him how very special he is to me.

Sarah Pence and Elijah

I REPLACED a six-foot Swedish husband with a five-pound dog. I hadn't intended to. In fact, I never liked dogs. I was afraid of them. No matter what the size, I asked friends to put "Buster" in the garage when I visited. So it's ironic that when my marriage was rockiest, I got a dog. It was one of the sanest things I'd done in years.

Even in the sleazy surroundings of the Los Angeles Dog and Reptile Farm, I knew what I'd name the smelly Yorkshire terrier who jumped into my lap: Framboise, a name to recall memories of childhood summers when my brother and I picked raspberries. I needed some of that happiness.

Because I didn't start out as a dog person, sometimes my attachment to Framboise embarrassed me. Loving a man or a child, yes, but a dog? And a dog small enough to tote about in a straw bag? Dr. Samuel Johnson's words reassured me: "There is nothing too little for so small a creature as man. It is by studying little things that we attain the great art of having as little misery and as much happiness as possible."

PHOTO: Daniel Martinez

Jo Giese and Framboise

MY LIVING ROOM is a constant battleground. Bronson and Honey Bear claim the couch as theirs and want access rights. I claim the couch is my territory, and so the battle ensues.

The final confrontation — Bronson admits defeat and Honey Bear tries to be inconspicuous.

Mary Zucosky with Bronson and Honey Bear

WHISKEY, a.k.a. the Whisk, Little Woo. Born and lived in Florence, Italy. Was fluent in English and Italian. Whiskey was a bona-fido member of the Pan Am Clipper Club. She ate in many of Italy's finest restaurants and was a favorite at Harry's Bar, Florence. The Whisk spent her golden years with me in Boston, leaving the jet-set life of an Italian *principessa* for Beacon Hill and weekends in Vermont. Sunday cruises on Granny Pond were one of her favorite postbrunch activities.

PHOTO: © Steve Schmitt

Anne Schmitt and Whiskey

MAX AND ARABELLA run the show. I try, honestly I try, to keep them off the furniture. God knows what they do during the day when I am at work. They know, I know they know, they are not to get on the furniture. I tell them all the time! And especially my bed. Arabella's the worst. Even when I'm home, she'll sneak very quietly and slowly up the stairs and slither her way up onto my bed. When I realize it I'll yell, and she'll come down looking very guilty, with her head low, and glare at me out of the corner of her eye.

It isn't that they're stupid or hard to train, quite the opposite. They are just very manipulative and seductive. Why, they can almost get onto the bed when I'm in it and I won't know it. So, I try, honestly I try, but I always give in.

Susan Quinby with Max and Arabella

I PROTECT CANOLLI from big dogs and tough cats. In return my furry red-headed protector alerts me to things she senses are not quite right. She is my pumpkin pie and honey bear with an olive nose and cupped ears. She has brought laughter and joy into my life — the greatest gifts of all.

PHOTO: © Ann Meredith

Laura Camodeca and Canolli

I DON'T CONSIDER THE DOGS as my pets, it's more that we're all fortunate to be sharing the same rocky road. Their luxuries in life are many — they *are* lucky dogs — and my unceasing joy lies in being fortunate enough to see the call of the wild in their eyes every now and then.

Eve S. Minson with Dakota, Tundra, and Sterling

OH MY WALLY, my little Liebchen, my little toadster, my little best boy. He is a hard-working farm boy, loves the beach, and loves his mummy as much as she loves him. That's my Wally, my little lipster man.

PHOTO: © Barbara Hadden

Cathy Haskell and Wally

I FOUND JOHANN in the summer of 1976. He had been dumped on the median strip on the Eisenhower expressway in Chicago. He was in shock, starving, and dehydrated. My brother and I managed to get him to the vet in time to save him. We had ten years together after that, all of them spent possessively devoted to each other.

This picture was taken the winter of 1980 in Boston, when Johann and I had just returned from a disastrous year in Fort Lauderdale. We were both very happy to be little kids playing in the snow again.

Robin Bestler and Johann

Never lonely.

Karen Jerome with Omar and Bern